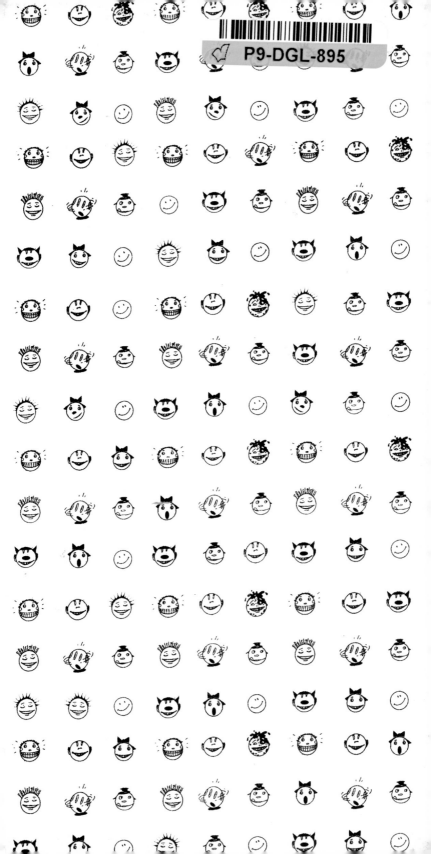

P9-DGL-895

for Kati — I.B.

This is a Borzoi Book published by Alfred A. Knopf, Inc.

Alfred A. Knopf is indebted to the Carl Sandburg Family Trust, Maurice C.
Greenbaum and Philip G. Carson Trustees, for permission to publish these
poems and is grateful for the cooperation of the University of Illinois Library at
Urbana-Champaign, the repository of the physical documents.

www.randomhouse.com/kids

Library of Congress Cataloging-in-Publication Data
Sandburg, Carl, 1878-1967.
Poems for children nowhere near old enough to vote / by Carl Sandburg ;
illustrated by Istvan Banyai; Compiled and with an introduction by George and
Willene Hendrick.
p. cm.
Summary: A collection of previously unpublished poems by the well-known
American poet Carl Sandburg about such familiar objects and ideas as the
moon, manners, eyes, necks, pencils, and clouds.
ISBN 0-679-88990-6 (trade). — ISBN 0-679-98990-0 (lib. bdg.)
1. Children's poetry, American. [1. American poetry.]
I. Banyai, Istvan, ill. II. Title.
PS3537.A618A6 1999
811'.52—dc21
98-39551

Printed in the United States of America

10 9 8 7 6 5 4 3 2 1

First Edition

CARL SANDBURG

P O E M S

F O R

C H I L D R E N

POEMS FOR CHILDREN

NOWHERE NEAR OLD ENOUGH TO VOTE

ILLUSTRATIONS BY ISTVAN BANYAI

COMPILED AND WITH AN INTRODUCTION BY
GEORGE AND WILLENE HENDRICK

ALFRED A. KNOPF ⟩⟩ NEW YORK

Poets are sometimes forgetful. They write poems, and if these verses are ahead of their time or quite unlike their other poetry, they put them aside for another day. They file them, and there they stay, the paper turning yellow with age, and the poems are forgotten. Something like this seems to have happened with Carl Sandburg's collection *Poems for Children Nowhere Near Old Enough to Vote.*

Sixty years ago or so, when the Sandburg family lived in Harbert, Michigan, near Chicago, Sandburg wrote a whole series of poems primarily for children. No doubt they provided moments of fun as he read them to his wife and his grown daughters, for the poems could amuse adults, too, as later on they would entertain his own grandchildren.

"Who was Carl Sandburg?" you ask. He was born to poor Swedish immigrants in Galesburg, Illinois, in 1878. His father worked as a blacksmith for the railroad and was paid fourteen cents an hour. Sandburg was a fun-loving, questioning, dreamy boy who always wanted to know the whys and wherefores of things. He was forced by family poverty to leave school after the eighth grade, and for several years he worked at odd jobs. The Spanish-American War of 1898 changed his life. As a veteran of that war, he was able to enter Lombard College in his hometown. In his four years there (1898–1902) he received a fine education, he read widely, he discovered he could write, and he became determined to be a poet. After several years, while he tried various forms of writing, he and his wife and children settled in Chicago, where he worked as a newspaper reporter. He still loved poetry, though, and constantly worked at writing his verses. He achieved national fame in 1916, when he published his first major book, *Chicago Poems.*

Sandburg published many volumes of poetry, but he had other books to write: "Rootabaga" stories for children, a collection of

American songs, his famous six-volume biography of Abraham Lincoln, and his autobiography, the story of his growing up in a small town. Always, he wrote straight to the people; he wanted everyone, child or adult, to understand his writing.

Prizes and awards came his way, but Sandburg remained a man of the people. For forty years, he roamed the country performing his unusual concerts: reading his poetry and his stories for children, playing his guitar and singing American folksongs, and sprinkling in comic comments here and there. When he died in 1967, he was one of this country's most distinguished literary figures.

Sandburg's papers and books—tons of them—have been deposited in the library of the University of Illinois at Urbana-Champaign, and among the thousands of pages of his manuscripts, we have found these poems, filed and forgotten. They now appear in print for the first time, superbly illustrated by Istvan Banyai. He has shaped the poems, and the lines and pictures run and hop and skip across the page. He has, as Sandburg himself had, a comic imagination: a chair crosses its legs, like a father relaxing with the evening newspaper after a hard day's work; a line about stumbling wavers, causing a stumble, even a fall. Banyai has put pictures together with words and sounds in new ways.

Sandburg liked to write stories and poems for children, for he knew that children love the sound of words just as he did. He was a jokester and liked to write funny, quirky poems about simple things: eggs and buttons, chairs, pencils, and clouds. He liked to write about the inexplicable mysteries of the world and the universe, for he knew that "what can be explained is not poetry."

Sandburg followed his imagination wherever it took him. *Poems for Children Nowhere Near Old Enough to Vote* invites the young—and the young at heart—to do the same.

George and Willene Hendrick
March 1999

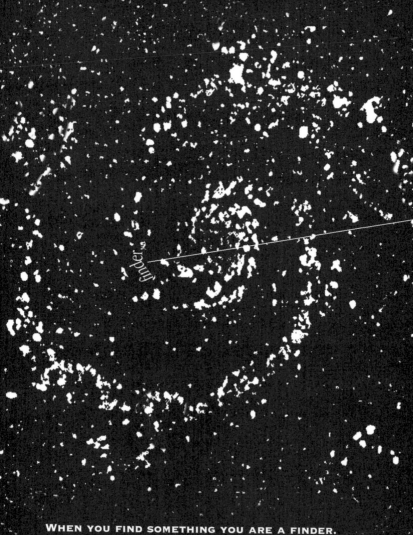

WHEN YOU FIND SOMETHING YOU ARE A FINDER.

WHEN YOU KEEP SOMETHING YOU ARE A KEEPER.

WHEN YOU GIVE SOMETHING YOU ARE A GIVER.

WHEN YOU LOSE SOMETHING YOU ARE A LOSER.

SO LONG AS YOU LIVE—EVERY MINUTE AND SECOND

AND CLOCK-TICK OF YOUR LIFE—YOU ARE EITHER

A FINDER, KEEPER, GIVER, LOSER.

When you find something you are a finder. When you keep something you are a keeper. When you give something you are a giver. When you lose something you are a loser. So long as you live—every minute and second and clock-tick of your life—you are either a finder, keeper, giver, loser.

FINDERS KEEPERS

Egos and Buttons

Eggs may speak to buttons—

that is correct.

Buttons, however, must not speak to eggs.

Not unless an egg needs a button.

Then the button may say to the egg,

"Can I be of any help to you?"

Can I be of
any help to you?

Nobody

Nobody is whoever comes into a room and it is still empty.

Nobody is who is in a room when everybody goes away.

Nobody is anybody so hard to see that you can't see him.

Nobody is whoever goes away so fast you can't see him and comes back the same way.

Nobody went upstairs and who came down? Nobody.

Nobody is yourself when you feel like nothing, like a naught, like a cipher, like a zero, like the letter **O**.

Nobodies bother nobodies.

MANNERS

MANNERS IS HOW TO BEHAVE.

MANNERS IS WHEN YOU KNOW HOW TO EAT WITHOUT
BEING BASHFUL.

MANNERS IS NOT AFRAID OF WHAT YOU ARE WEARING.

MANNERS IS LIKE A MAN TIPS HIS HAT WHEN HE
MEETS A LADY.

MANNERS IS "EXCUSE ME" OR "I BEG YOUR PARDON"
INSTEAD OF "HOW DO YOU GET THERE?" OR
"I'LL KNOCK YOUR BLOCK OFF."

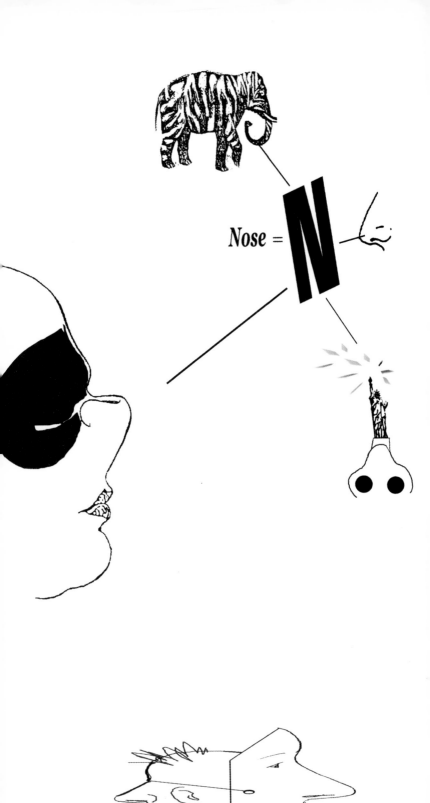

Nose = **N**

The nose is to breathe with and smell with.

Eyes need two and ears need two but one nose
is enough if it has two nostrils.

The nose fits better on the front of the face
than the back of the head.

The nose is to find to blow with the
handkerchief.

Noses come in different shapes and change
very little.

Each nose tells its own story.

Some noses are very independent.

EARS

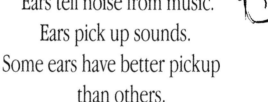

Ears are put on to stay.
We could wash the ears better
if we could take them off.
Ears hear better than the nose.
Ears listen for what comes.
Ears tell noise from music.
Ears pick up sounds.
Some ears have better pickup
than others.

: M U S I C :

Music is when your ears like what they hear,

Music is why voices you like to listen to.

Music for you   is   anything   you   hear

Music is any sound to go on and on.

want

you

that clicks w i t h you.

Music is when your ears like what they hear.

Music is any voices you like to listen to.

Music is any sound you want to go on and on.

Music for you is anything you hear that clicks

with you.

Necks

The neck is to wash clean every day.

The neck holds the  head on.

When you look up or look back, the neck

stretches.

Some necks are longer than others.

The longer the neck, the more there is to

wash every day.

Rubber necks are for dolls and dummies.

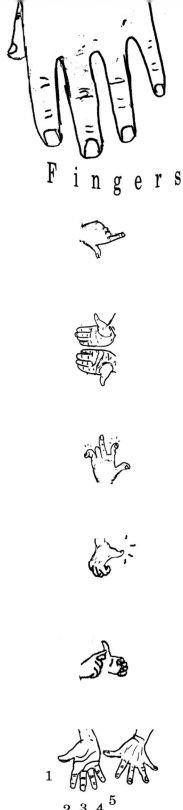

F i n g e r s

1
2 3 4 5

Each finger has its secrets.

The pointing finger is best at pointing.

Crook one finger and all the other fingers
       want to crook.

Bend one finger back and all the other fingers
       watch what happens.

Thumbs understand the fingers better than the
       fingers understand the thumb.

Sometimes the fingers feel sorry the thumb is
       not a finger.

The thumb is needed more often than any of the
       fingers.

Look close at any thumb and you see it is
       not proud.

Each finger has two knuckles, a thumb only one knuckle,
       and they need each other.

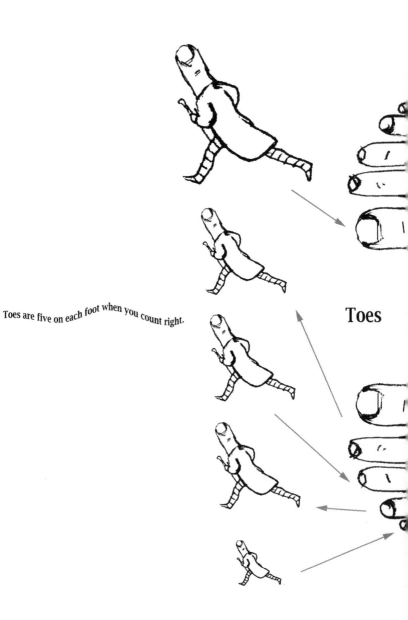

Toes are five on each foot when you count right.

Toes

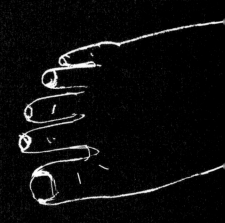

Toes are to wash when you take a bath.
Toes are to count to see how many.
Toes are five on each foot when you count right.
Right foot toes belong on the right foot.
Left foot toes belong on the left foot.
The big toe is the thumb of the foot.
All the other toes worry about the little toe.
The big toe likes itself very well.

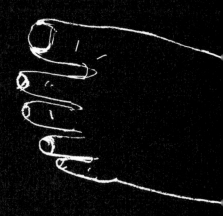

Stumbling is where you walk and find you are not walking.

Stumbling is where you find yourself spread on

the ground, instead of standing on your feet.

Stumbling is where your feet try to make a fool of you.

Stumbling is to go where you are not looking when you mean to go where you are looking.

Stumbling is to get your feet mixed so you go down.

Stumblers are two kinds, those who laugh and those who cry.

Stumblers are two kinds, those who come up quick and those who say, "Where am I?"

If you never want to stumble, be a fish or a bird.

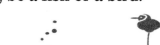

Pencils

Pencils are to hold when you write.
Pencils come loose unless you hold them.
One pencil writes many thousand words, if
    you know the words.
Pencils too pointed break their points and
    then laugh at you.
Blunt pencils write big long words for you
    even if the words mean nothing.
Proud pencils get furious waiting to be sharpened.
Long pencils say, "I will write a little book for you
    if you will find the little words."
Short pencil stubs say, "I write and I forget and
    leave it to the paper to remember."
Pencils in pockets and boxes shove each other and
    nearly come to fighting.
They wait to be found before they write again—the
    lost pencils.

C l o c k s

9

Clocks tell time by their faces.
Clocks go on whoever is looking.
Clocks tell when to get up.
Clocks stay where put.
Clocks never argue.
Clocks are the same night and day.
A stopped clock is right twice in
          twenty-four hours.
Clocks make wishes but no one knows
          what clocks wish.

Clocks make wishes but no one knows what clocks wish. Clocks make wishes but no one knows what clocks wish.

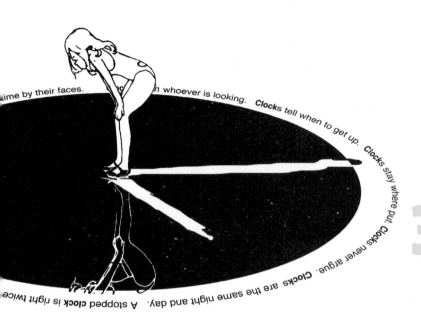

...ime by their faces. ...n whoever is looking. **Clock**s tell when to get up. **Clock**s stay where put. **Clock**s never argue. **Clock**s are the same night and day. A stopped **clock** is right twice

3

Clouds

Clouds are sky fluff. Clouds go by and come back. Clouds keep changing. Clouds cover the sun, the moon, the stars. Clouds make themselves into many shapes.

Sky

The sky is for birds to go up in.
The sky is as far as the moon, the stars, the sun.

The sky is higher than any mountain.

The sky is worth looking at.

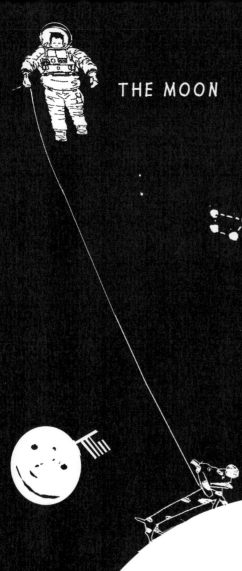

THE MOON

The moon is a dish of light.

The moon looks dirty with smoke and cloud wisps,
then changes till it looks washed and wiped.

The moon is a big penny got lost in the sky
one windy night.

The baby moon sings low, sings soft.

The harvest moon grins "Howdy."

The half moon says neither Yes nor No.

The lonesome moon talks to the lonesome
child saying, "Me too, me too."

The silver moon seems cold, not shivering but
chilly.

The moon is a looking glass you see your face
in if you climb high enough.

The peeping moon jumps out from clouds and goes
back.

The rising moon dares you to push it down.

The rising moon can't help laughing a little as
it says, "I don't know why I do this over and over
always the same way."

The full moon says it is good to be full and he
would be sorry for the empty if he was empty himself.

The late setting moon says, "I forgot something
and I'll be back when I remember what it was."

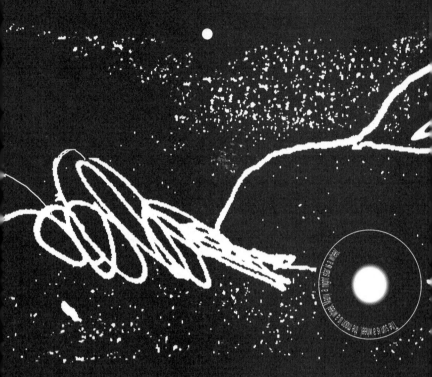

The sun is a wheel, the moon is a wheel. How many kinds of wheels?

Think About Wheels

THINK ABOUT WHEELS ANY TIME YOU LIKE.

ANY LITTLE WHEEL YOU SEE IS WORTH LOOKING AT.

THE SUN IS A WHEEL, THE MOON IS A WHEEL.

MANY A NIGHT STAR IS A WHEEL.

AND IN YOUR HEAD, IN MANY LITTLE PLACES BEHIND

YOUR BLINKING WONDERFUL EYES, YOU CAN FIND,

IF YOU TRY, TEN THOUSAND WHEELS WITHIN WHEELS.